Easter

Lori Dittmer

CREATIVE EDUCATION • CREATIVE PAPERBACKS

Published by Creative Education and Creative Paperbacks
P.O. Box 227, Mankato, Minnesota 56002
Creative Education and Creative Paperbacks
are imprints of The Creative Company
www.thecreativecompany.us

Design by Ellen Huber; production by Colin O'Dea
Art direction by Rita Marshall

Photographs by Getty Images (Dieter Hopf, Maximilian
Stock Ltd./Photolibrary), iStockphoto (bonetta, capdesign,
CaroleGomez, fzant, gchutka, imamember, jenifoto, matt_
scherf, mediaphotos, MediaProduction, MichaelLoeffler,
robertsrob, Sasiistock, SQUAMISH, SvitlanaMartyn,
SVproduction, ultramarine5)

Library of Congress Cataloging-in-Publication Data Names:
Dittmer, Lori, author.
Title: Easter / Lori Dittmer.
Series: Seedlings.
Includes index.
Summary: A kindergarten-level introduction to Easter,
covering the holiday's history, popular traditions, and such
defining symbols as baby animals and eggs.
Identifiers: LCCN 2019053291 / ISBN 978-1-64026-328-4
(hardcover) / ISBN 978-1-62832-860-8 (pbk) / ISBN
978-1-64000-458-0 (eBook)
Subjects: LCSH: Easter—Juvenile literature.
Classification: LCC GT4935.D57 2020 / DDC 394.261—dc23

CCSS: RI.K.1, 2, 3, 4, 5, 6, 7;
RI.1.1, 2, 3, 4, 5, 6, 7; RF.K.1, 3; RF.1.1

TABLE OF CONTENTS

Hello, Easter!

Easter celebrates new life.

It happens in late
March or April.

Baby animals are
signs of new life.
Eggs are, too.

Lilies and other flowers bloom.

More than 2,000 years ago, Jesus Christ was put to death. He was buried for three days. Christians believe he lived again on Easter.

Early church leaders
set the date.

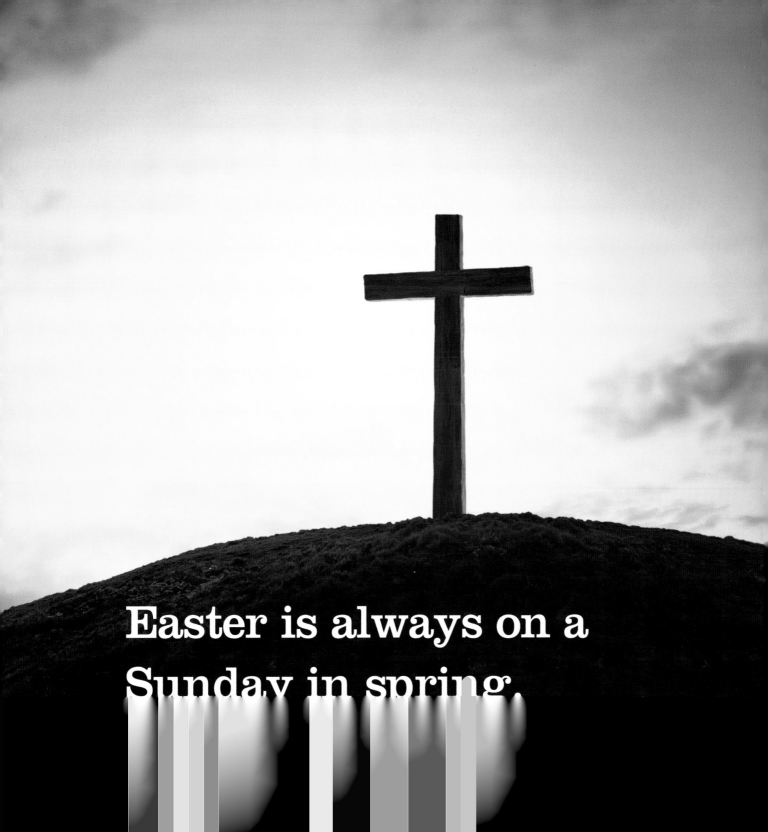

Easter is always on a
Sunday in spring.

Families gather for special meals. They might have ham and hot cross buns. They eat jelly beans and chocolate eggs, too.

Kids carry baskets.
They hunt for
Easter eggs.

Many Christians go to church.

Goodbye, Easter!

lilies

Easter basket

eggs

rabbit

Words to Know

Jesus Christ: the man whom Christians believe was the son of God

signs: things that show something is coming

Read More

Grack, Rachel. *Easter*.
Minneapolis: Bellwether Media, 2017.

Sebra, Richard. *It's Easter!*
Minneapolis: Lerner, 2017.

Websites

DKfindout: Easter
https://www.dkfindout.com/us/more-find-out/festivals-and
-holidays/easter/
Read more about Easter, and take a quiz about holidays.

Ducksters: Holidays – Easter
https://www.ducksters.com/holidays/easter.php
Learn about the history and traditions of Easter.

Index